Written by David Yale

Illustrated by US Illustrations

2025

First printing, 2025.

To my kids, Griffin, Jared and Cameron,
for bringing out the kid in me...

Mikey's having a visitor today.

Mikey and Poppy are going to play!

"Come find me, Poppy."

"Where's Mikey?"

Poppy calls out: "Is Mikey under the couch?"

We hear a reply from somewhere:

"No."

no

"Is Mikey behind the curtain?"

"No."

no

"Is Mikey behind the chair ?"

"No."

no

"Is Mikey behind the bathroom door?"

"No."

no

"Is Mikey behind the grandfather clock?"

"No."

no

"I give up Mikey. I can't find you!"

But wait, Poppy hears laughter...
but from where?

"Is Mikey under the dining room table?"

"YES!"

"OK Poppy, now you hide and I'll find you!"

The End